Songs And Dances Of Scotland

Arranged for
Recorder, Flute & Penny Whistle

Selected and arranged by Liz Thomson

WISE PUBLICATIONS
London/New York/Sydney

Exclusive Distributors:
MUSIC SALES LIMITED
8/9 Frith Street, London, W1V 5TZ, England
MUSIC SALES CORPORATION
257 Park Avenue South, New York, N.Y. 10010, U.S.A.
MUSIC SALES PTY. LIMITED
120 Rothschild Avenue, Rosebery, NSW 2018, Australia

This book © Copyright 1982 by
Wise Publications
ISBN 0.7119.0100.7
Order No. AM 31410

Designed by Howard Brown
Cover illustration by Tony Meeuwissen

Music Sales' complete catalogue lists thousands of
titles and is free from your local music book shop,
or direct from Music Sales Limited.
Please send a cheque/postal order for £1.50 for postage to
Music Sales Limited, 8/9 Frith Street, London, W1V 5TZ.

Printed and bound in Great Britain by
J.B. Offset Printers (Marks Tey) Limited, Marks Tey.

Farewell Tae Tarwathie

Traditional

Slowly, with feeling

1. Fare - weel tae Tar - wath - ie, a - dieu Mor - mond Hill, And the dear land o'

Cri - mond I bid ye fare - weel. I'm bound out for Green - land and

rea - dy to sail, In hopes to find rich - es in hunt - ing— the whale.

2. Adieu to my comrades, for a while we must pairt,
   And likewise the dear lass wha fair won my hairt;
   The cold ice of Greenland my love will not chill,
   And the longer my absence, more loving she feel.

3. Our ship is weel rigged and she's ready to sail,
   Our crew they are anxious to follow the whale;
   Where the icebergs do float and' the stormy winds blaw,
   Where the land and the ocean is covered wi' snaw.

4. The cold coast of Greenland is barren and bare,
   No seed-time nor harvest is ever known there;
   And the birds here sing sweetly on mountain and dale,
   But there isna a birdie to sing to the whale.

5. There is no habitation for a man to live there,
   And the King of that country is the fierce Greenland bear;
   And there'll be no temptation to tarry lang there,
   Wi' our ship bumper full we will homeward repair.

An Eriskay Love Lilt

Words & Music Kenneth MacLeod and Marjory Kennedy-Fraser

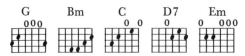

With tender passion

Bheir mi ò - ro bhan o Bheir mi ò - ro bhan
Vair me o - ro van o Vair me o - ro van

i Bheir mi o - ru o ho 'S mi tha bron - ach's tu'm
ee Vair me o - ru o ho Sad am I with - out

dhith._____ 'Siom-adh oidh - che fliuch is
thee._____ When I'm lone - ly dear white
Fad - a siar air agh-aidh

fuar Ghabh mi cuairt is mi leam fhin, Gus an d'rain - ig mi'n
heart Black the night or wild the sea, By love's light my foot
cuain 'Se mo dhuan - sa Cruit-mo - chridh, Guth mo luaidh anns gach

t-àit Fai'n robh gradh geal mo chridh. Bheir mi o_____ ro bhan o Bheir mi
finds The old path - way to thee. Vair me o_____ ro van o Vair me
stuaidh 'Ga mo nuall - an gu tir.

D7

o_____ ro bhan i Bheir mi o ru o ho 'Smi tha
o_____ ro van ee Vair me o ru o ho Sad am

G   C   G

bròn - ach's tu'm dhith._____   'Na mo
I   with-out   thee._____   Thou'rt the
                                            Gur tu

Bm   Em   Bm   D7

Chlàr - saich cha robh ceòl 'Na mo mheoir - ean cha robh àgh, Rinn do
mus - ic of my heart, Harp of joy, oh cruit mo chridh, Moon of
m'òig - e is mo rùn, Mo re - iùil thu anns an oidhch, Tha mo

G   C   G

phòg - sa mo leon, Fhuair mi Eol - as an dàin. Bheir mi o_____ ro bhan
guid - ance by night, Strength and light thou'rt to me. Vair me o_____ ro van
dhrùidh-eachd ad shùil, Tha mo chiurr - adh ad loinn.

D7

o Bheir mi o_____ ro bhan i Bheir mi o ru o
o Vair me o_____ ro van ee Vair me o ru o

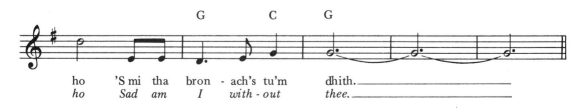

G   C   G

ho 'S mi tha bron - ach's tu'm dhith._____
ho Sad am I with - out thee._____

THE BONNIE LASS O'FYVIE-O

Traditional

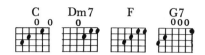

Moderately

1. There was a _____ troop o' I-rish Dra-goons Cam' a-

mar-chin' doon through_ Fy-vie-o, An' their cap-tain's fa'n in love wi' a

ve-ry bon-nie lass, An' her name it was ca'd_ pret-ty Peg-gy-o.

2. Noo there's mony a bonnie lass in the Howe o' Auchterless,
   There's mony a bonnie lass in the Garioch-o,
   There's mony a bonnie Jean in the toon o' Aiberdeen,
   But the floo'er o' them a' is in Fyvie-o.

3. Oh it's 'Come doon the stair, pretty Peggy, my dear,
   Oh come doon the stair, pretty Peggy-o,
   Oh come doon the stair, kame back your yellow hair,
   Tak' a last farewell o' your daddy-o.

4. 'For it's I'll gie ye ribbons for your bonnie gowden hair,
   I'll gie ye a necklace o' amber-o,
   I'll gie ye silken petticoats wi' flounces tae the knee
   If ye'll convoy me doon tae my chaumer-o.'

5. 'Oh I hae got ribbons for my bonnie gowden hair,
   An' I hae got a necklace o' amber-o
   An' I hae got petticoats befitting my degree,
   An' I'd scorn tae be seen in your chaumer-o.'

6. 'What would your mammy think if she heard the guineas clink
   An' the hautboys a-playin' afore you-o?
   What would your mammy think when she heard the guineas clink,
   An' kent you had married a sodger-o?'

7. 'Oh a sodger's wife I never shall be,
   A sodger shall never enjoy me-o.
   For I never do intend to go to a foreign land,
   So I never shall marry a sodger-o.'

8. 'A sodger's wife ye never shall be,
   For ye'll be the captain's lady-o,
   An' the regiments shall stand wi' their hats intae their hands,
   An' they'll bow in the presence o' my Peggy-o.'

9. 'It's braw, aye, it's braw a captain's lady tae be,
   It's braw tae be a captain's lady-o.
   It's braw tae rant an' rove an' tae follow at his word,
   An' tae march when your captain he is ready-o.'

10. But the Colonel he cries 'Now mount, boys, mount!'
    The captain he cries 'Oh tarry-o.
    Oh gang nae awa' for anither day or twa,
    Till we see if this bonnie lass will marry-o.'

11. It was early next morning that we rode awa'
    An' oh but oor captain was sorry-o.
    The drums they did beat owre the bonnie braes o' Gight
    An' the band played The Lowlands o' Fyvie-o.

12. Lang ere we wan intae auld Meldrum toon
    It's we had oor captain to carry-o.
    An' lang ere we wan intae bonnie Aiberdeen,
    It's we had oor captain tae bury-o.

13. Green grow the birk upon bonnie Ythanside
    An' law lies the lawlands o' Fyvie-o.
    The captain's name was Ned an' he died for a maid;
    He died for the bonnie lass o' Fyvie-o.

THE BLANTYRE EXPLOSION

Traditional

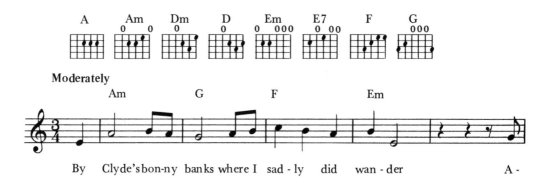

Moderately

By Clyde's bon-ny banks where I sad-ly did wan-der A-

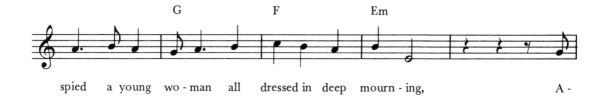

-mong the pit heaps as___ eve-ning drew nigh, I

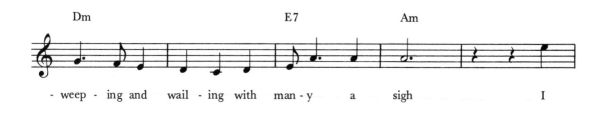

spied a young wo-man all dressed in deep mourn-ing, A-

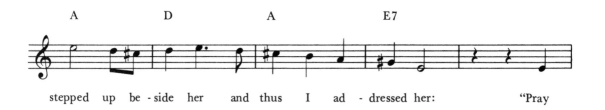

-weep-ing and wail-ing with man-y a sigh I

stepped up be-side her and thus I ad-dressed her: "Pray

tell me the cause of your troub-le and pain."

Weep - ing and sigh - ing, at last she made an - swer: "John - ny

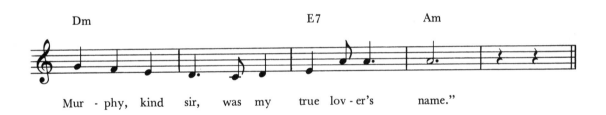

Mur - phy, kind sir, was my true lov - er's name."

2. 'Twenty-one years of age, full of youth and good looking,
   To work down the mines of High Blantyre he came.
   The wedding was fixed, all the guests were invited
   That calm summer evening young Johnny was slain.
   The explosion was heard, all the women and children
   With pale anxious faces they haste to the mine.
   When the truth was made known, the hills rang with their mourning,
   Three-hundred-and-ten young miners were slain."

   Now husbands and wives and sweethearts and brothers,
   That Blantyre explosion they'll never forget;
   And all the young miners that hear my sad story,
   Shed a tear for the victims who're laid to their rest.

The Road To The Isles

Words by Kenneth MacLeod Music Arr: Patuffa Kennedy-Fraser

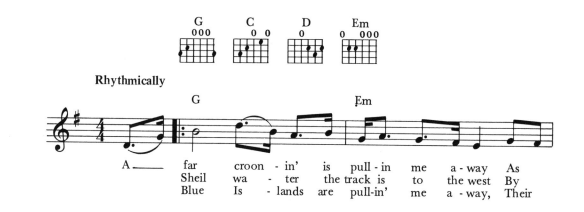

Rhythmically

A — far croon - in' is pull - in me a - way As
Sheil wa - ter the track is to the west By
Blue Is - lands are pull-in' me a - way, Their

take I wi' my cro-mak to the road, The — far Cool - ins are
Aill - ort and by Mo - rar to the sea, The — cool cres - ses I am
laugh-ter puts the leap up - on the lame, The — blue Is - lands from the

put - tin' love on me As step I wi' the sun - light for my load.
think-in' o' for pluck, And brac-ken for a wink on Moth - er knee. } Sure, by
Sker - ries to the Lews, Wi' heath-er hon - ey taste up - on each name.

Tum - mel and Loch Ran-noch and Loch - a - ber I will go, By —

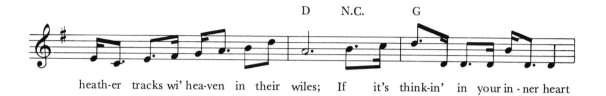

heath-er tracks wi' hea-ven in their wiles; If it's think-in' in your in - ner heart

brag - gart's in my step, You've ne - ver smelt the tan - gle o' the

Isles. Oh, the far Cool - ins are put-tin' love on me, As

step I wi' my cro - mak to the Isles. It's by Isles.
It's the

WALY WALY

Traditional

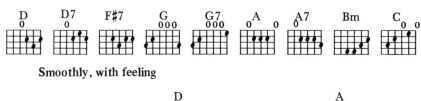

Smoothly, with feeling

O, wa - ly, wa - ly up the bank, And wa - ly,

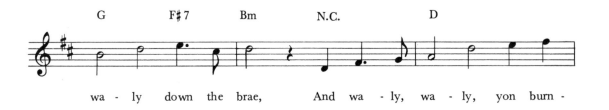

wa - ly down the brae, And wa - ly, wa - ly, yon burn -

- side, Where I and my love wont to gae! I leaned my

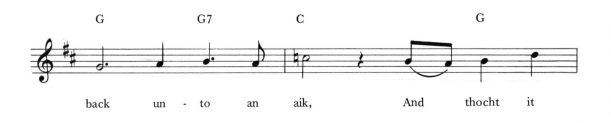

back un - to an aik, And thocht it

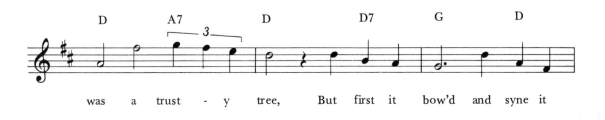

was a trust - y tree, But first it bow'd and syne it

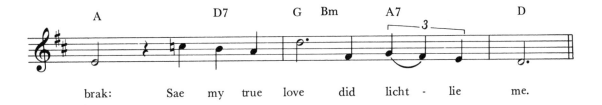

brak: Sae   my   true   love   did   licht - lie   me.

2. O waly, waly but love be bonnie
   A little time while it is new,
   But when it's auld it waxes cauld
   And fades away like morning dew.
   O, wherefore should I busk my heid,
   Or wherefore should I kame my hair?
   For my true-love has me forsook,
   And says he'll never love me mair.

3. Now Arthur's seat shall be my bed,
   The sheets shall ne'er be pressed by me,
   St. Anton's Well shall be my drink,
   Since my true-love has forsaken me.
   Martinmas wind, when wilt thou blaw,
   And shake the green leaves aff the tree?
   O gentle death when wilt thou come?
   For of my life I am wearie.

4. 'Tis not the frost that freezes fell,
   Nor blawing snaw's inclemencie;
   'Tis not sic cauld that mak's me cry,
   But my love's heart's grown cauld to me.
   When we came in by Glasgow toun,
   We were a comely sicht to see;
   My love was clad in the black velvet,
   And I mysel' in cramasie.

5. But had I wist before I kiss't
   That love had been sae ill to win,
   I'd lock'd my heart in a case of gold,
   And pinn'd it wi' a siller pin.
   Oh, oh, if my young babe were born,
   And set upon the nurse's knee,
   And I mysel' were dead and gone,
   And the green grass growin' ower me!

ROBIN ADAIR

Traditional

Quite Slowly

1. What's this dull town to me? Ro - bin's not here. What was't I wish'd to see? What wish'd to hear Where's all the joy and mirth Made this town a Heav'n on earth? Oh! they're all fled with thee, Ro - bin A - dair.

2. What made th'as - sem - bly shine? Ro - bin A - dair. What made the Ball so fine? Ro - bin A - dair. And when the play was o'er, What made my heart so sore? Oh! it was part - ing with Ro - bin A - dair.

3. But now thou'rt cold to me, Ro - bin A - dair. But now thou'rt cold to me, Ro - bin A - dair. Yet him I loved so well Still in my heart shall dwell; Oh! I can ne'er for - get Ro - bin A - dair.

COMIN' THRO' THE RYE

Traditional

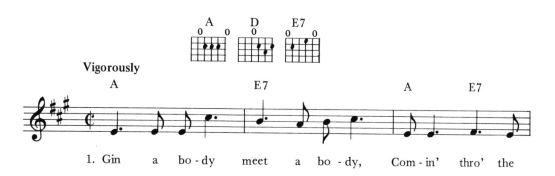

Vigorously

1. Gin a bo-dy meet a bo-dy, Com-in' thro' the

rye; Gin a bo-dy kiss a bo-dy, Need a bo-dy cry?

Ilk-a las-sie has her lad-die, Nane, they say, ha'e' I; Yet a' the lads they

smile at me, When com-in' thro' the rye. rye. A - rye.

2. Gin a body meet a body, Comin' frae the toon;
   Gin a body meet a body, Need a body froon?

CHORUS

3. Amang the train there is a swain I dearly lo'e mysel',
   But what's his name, or what's his hame, I dinna care to tell.

CHORUS

THE TARTAN

Words by Sydney Bell Music by Kenneth McKellar

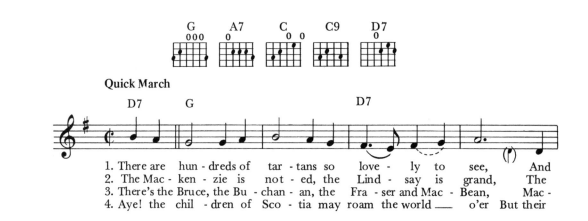

Quick March

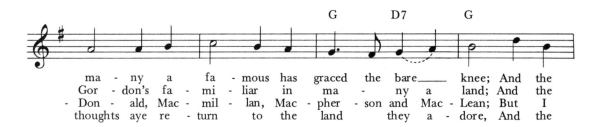

1. There are hun - dreds of tar - tans so love - ly to see, And
2. The Mac - ken - zie is not - ed, the Lind - say is grand, The
3. There's the Bruce, the Bu - chan - an, the Fra - ser and Mac - Bean, Mac -
4. Aye! the chil - dren of Sco - tia may roam the world ___ o'er But their

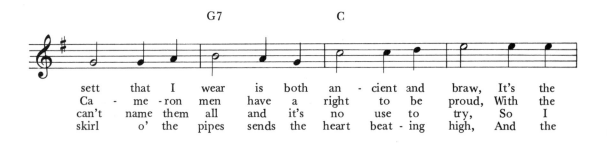

ma - ny a fa - mous has graced the bare___ knee; And the
Gor - don's fa - mi - liar in ma - ny a land; And the
- Don - ald, Mac - mil - lan, Mac - pher - son and Mac - Lean; But I
thoughts aye re - turn to the land they a - dore, And the

sett that I wear is both an - cient and braw, It's the
Ca - me - ron men have a right to be proud, With the
can't name them all and it's no use to try, So I
skirl o' the pipes sends the heart beat - ing high, And the

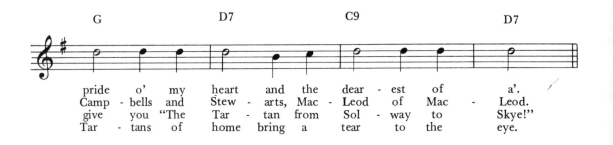

pride o' my heart and the dear - est of a'.
Camp - bells and Stew - arts, Mac - Leod of Mac - Leod.
give you "The Tar - tan from Sol - way to Skye!"
Tar - tans of home bring a tear to the eye.

Then it's Hey! for THE TAR - TAN and Ho! for THE

TAR - TAN! The stamp o' the Hie - lands from Skye to Dun -

- dee; And it's proud I am bear - ing THE TAR - TAN I'm

wear - ing, The pride o' my Clan and THE TAR - TAN for

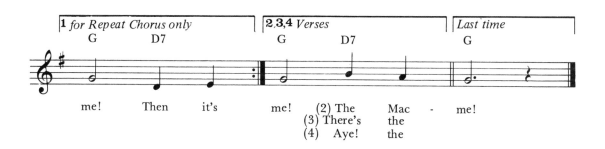

me! Then it's me! (2) The Mac - me!
(3) There's the
(4) Aye! the

17

THE CRUEL MOTHER

Traditional

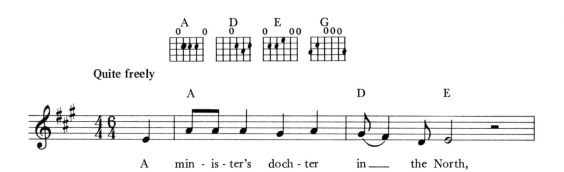

Quite freely

A min - is - ter's doch - ter in ___ the North,

Hey, the rose and the lin - sie O, She's fa'-en in love wi' her

faith - er's clerk, Doon by the green-wood sid - ie, O. ___

2. She's coorted him a year and a day,
   Till her the young man did betray.

3. She leaned her back against a tree,
   And there the tear did blin' her e'e.

4. She leaned her back against a thorn,
   And there twa bonnie boys has she born.

5. She's ta'en the napkin frae her neck,
   And made to them a winding sheet.

6. She's ta'en oot her wee penknife,
   And quickly twined them o' their life.

7. She's laid them 'neath a marble stane,
   Thinking to gang a maiden hame.

8. She looked ower her faither's wa',
   And she's seen they twa bonnie boys at the ba'.

9. "O, bonnie bairns, gin ye were mine,
   I would dress ye in the silk sae fine."

10. "O, cruel mither, when we were thine,
    We didna see ocht o' the silk sae fine."

11. "O, bonnie bairns, come tell to me,
    Whit kind o' a deith I'll hae to dee."

12. "Seven year a fish in the flood,
    Seven year a bird in the wood.

13. Seven years a tongue to the warning bell,
    Seven years in the caves o' hell."

14. "Welcome, welcome, fish in the flood,
    Welcome, welcome, bird in the wood.

15. Welcome, tongue to the warning bell
    But God keep me frae the caves o' Hell."

BYRNES HORNPIPE

Traditional

WILL YE NO COME BACK AGAIN

Traditional

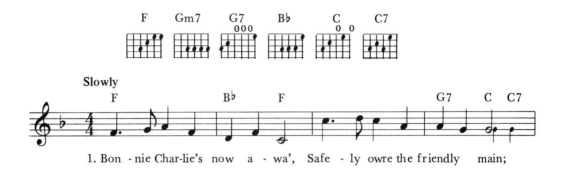

Slowly

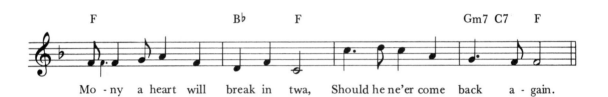

1. Bon - nie Char-lie's now a - wa', Safe - ly owre the friendly main;

Mo - ny a heart will break in twa, Should he ne'er come back a - gain.

CHORUS

Will ye no come back a - gain? Will ye no come back _ a - gain?

Bet - ter lo'ed ye can - na be, Will ye no come back a - gain?

2. Sweet's the laverock's note and lang,
   Lilting wildly up the glen;
   But aye to me he sings ae sang
   "Will ye no come back again?"

CHORUS

ROTHSAY-O

Traditional

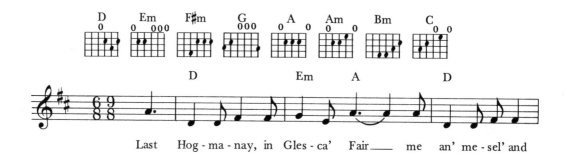

Last Hog - ma - nay, in Gles - ca' Fair____ me an' me - sel' and

sev - eral mair_____ All gaed off to hae a wee tair_____ To

spend the nicht in Roth - say - O_____ We start - ed off frae the

Broom - ie - law___ Baith hail and sleet and rain and snaw_____

For - ty min - utes aif - ter twa _____ We got the length of

Roth - say - O A dur - rum - a - doo - a - doo - a - day_____ A

dur - rum - a - doo - a - dad - dy - O_____ A dur - rum - a - doo - a -

- doo - a - day_____ The nicht we went to Roth - say - O

2. There was a lad called Ru'glen Will
   Whose regiment's lying at Barra Hill
   Gaed off wi' a tanner to get a gill
   Before we went to Rothsay-O
   Says he: I think I'd like to sing
   Says I: Ye'll nae dae sicca thing
   I'll clear the room and I'll mak' a ring
   And I'll fecht them all in Rothsay-O

CHORUS

3. In search of lodgings we did slide
   To get a place where we could bide
   There were just eighty-twa of us inside
   In a single room in Rothsay-O
   We all lay doon to get our ease
   When somebody happened for to sneeze
   And they wakened half a million fleas
   In a single room in Rothsay-O

CHORUS

4. There were several different types of bugs
   Some had feet like dyer's clugs
   An' they sat on the bed an' cockit their lugs
   An' cried: Hurrah for Rothsay-O
   O noo, says I, we'll have to 'lope
   So we went and joined the Band o' Hope
   But the pol-is wouldna let us stop
   Another nicht in Rothsay-O

CHORUS

THE FLOWERS O' THE FOREST

Traditional

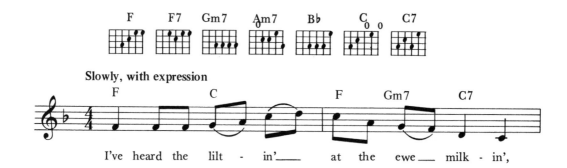

Slowly, with expression

I've heard the lilt - in'___ at the ewe ___ milk - in',

lass - es a lilt - in' be - fore ___ dawn of day. Now there's a moan - in' on

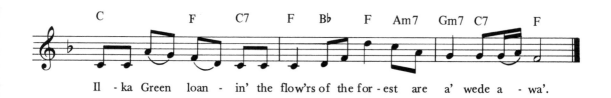

Il - ka Green loan - in' the flow'rs of the for - est are a' wede a - wa'.

2. At bughts in the mornin', nae blithe lads are scornin',
   Lassies are lanely, an' dowie, an' wae,
   Nae daffin', nae gabbin', but sighin' an' sabbin';
   Ilk ane lifts her laglin', an' hies her awa'.

3. We'll ha'e nae mair liltin' at the ewe milkin',
   Women an' bairns are heartless an' wae;
   Sighin' an' moanin' on Ilka Green loanin',
   The flowers o' the forest are a' wede awa'.

THE KEEL ROW

Traditional

SCOTLAND THE BRAVE

Traditional

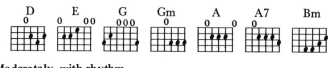

Moderately, with rhythm

MARY HAMILTON
Traditional

Word is to the kit-chen gone And word is to the hall, And word is up to Mad-am the Queen And that's the worst of all,

2nd & Others

1st verse only That Mar - y Ham-il-ton's borne a babe to the high-est Stu-art of all.

2. "Arise, arise, Mary Hamilton,
   Arise and tell to me,
   What thou hast done with thy wee babe
   I saw and heard weep by thee?"

3. "I put him in a tiny boat,
   And cast him out to sea,
   That he might sink or he might swim,
   But he'd never come back to me."

4. "Arise, arise, Mary Hamilton,
   Arise and come with me;
   There is a wedding in Glasgow town,
   This night we'll go and see."

5. She put not on her robes of black,
   Nor her robes of brown,
   But she put on her robes of white,
   To ride into Glasgow town.

6. And as she rode into Glasgow town,
   The city for to see,
   The bailiff's wife and the provost's wife
   Cried, "Ach, and alas for thee."

7. "Ah, you need not weep for me," she cried,
   "You need not weep for me;
   For had I not slain my own wee babe,
   This death I would not dee."

8. "Ah, little did my mother think
   When first she cradled me,
   The lands I was to travel in,
   And the death I was to dee."

9. "Last night I washed the Queen's feet,
   And put the gold in her hair,
   And the only reward I find for this,
   The gallows to be my share."

10. "Cast off, cast off my gown, she cried,
    "But let my petticoat be,
    And tie a napkin 'round my face;
    The gallows I would not see."

11. Then by and come the King Himself,
    Looked up with a pitiful eye,
    "Come down, come down, Mary Hamilton,
    Tonight, you'll dine with me."

12. "Ah, hold your tongue, my sovereign liege,
    And let your folly be;
    For if you'd a mind to save my life,
    You'd never have shamed me here."

13. "Last night there were four Marys,
    Tonight there'll be but three,
    There was Mary Beaton, and Mary Seton,
    And Mary Carmichael, and me."

THE MINGULAY BOAT SONG

Traditional

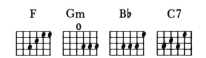

Rhythmically

CHORUS:

Hill you ho, boys: let her go boys; bring her head round, now all __ to

-geth-er. Hill you ho, boys; Let her go boys; Sail-ing home, home to Min-gu-

-lay.　　lay.　VERSE:　What care we though white __ the

Minch is? What care we for wind __ and weath-er? Let her

go boys! ev-'ry inch is wear-ing home, home to Min-gu-lay. Hill you

2. Wives are waiting on the bank, or
Looking sea-ward from the heather;
Pull her round boys! and we'll anchor,
Ere the sun sets at Mingulay.

LEEZIE LINDSAY

Traditional

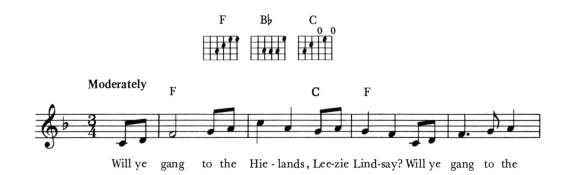

Moderately

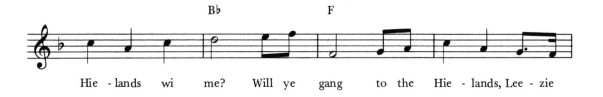

Will ye gang to the Hie-lands, Lee-zie Lind-say? Will ye gang to the

Hie-lands wi me? Will ye gang to the Hie-lands, Lee-zie

Lin-say, My pride and my dar-ling to___ be?

2. To gang to the Hielands, wi' you, sir,
   I dinna ken how that may be,
   For I ken nae the land that ye live in,
   Nor ken I the lad I'm gaun we.

3. O Leezie, lass, ye maun ken little,
   If sae ye dinna ken me;
   For my name is Lord Ronald MacDonald,
   A chieftain o' high degree.

4. She has kilted coats o' green satin
   She has kilted them up to the knee;
   An' she's off wi' Lord Ronald MacDonald,
   His bride and his darling to be.

AFTON WATER

Traditional

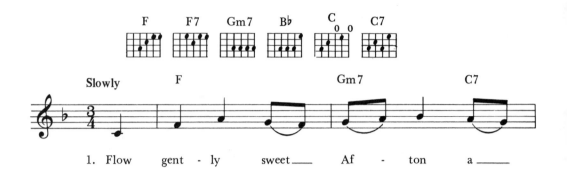

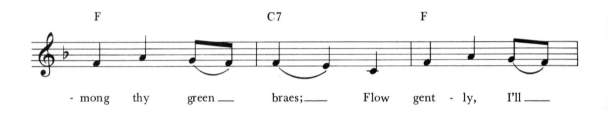

1. Flow gent - ly sweet___ Af - ton a___

- mong thy green___ braes;___ Flow gent - ly, I'll___

sing___ thee a___ song in___ thy___ praise. My___

Ma - ry's a___ sleep by thy mur - mur - ing___ stream,___ Flow

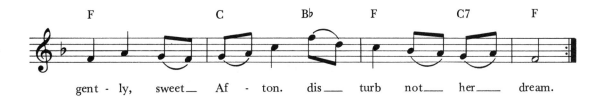

gent - ly, sweet__ Af - ton. dis __ turb not__ her__ dream.

2. Thou stock dove whose echo resounds thro' the glen,
   Ye wild whistling blackbirds in yon thorny den,
   Thou green crested lap wing, thy screaming forbear,
   I charge you disturb not my slumbering fair.

3. Thy crystal stream Afton, how lovely it glides
   And winds by the cot where my Mary resides!
   How wanton thy waters her snowy feet lave
   As, gath'ring sweet flow'rets she stems thy clear wave.

4. Flow gently, sweet Afton among thy green braes,
   Flow gently, sweet river, the theme of my lays:
   My Mary's asleep by thy murmuring stream,
   Flow gently, sweet Afton, disturb not her dream.

LAMENT OF FLORA MACDONALD

Traditional

With expression and flow (Guitar tacet)

ANNIE LAURIE

Traditional

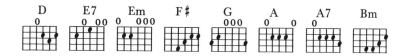

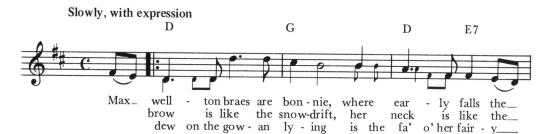

Slowly, with expression

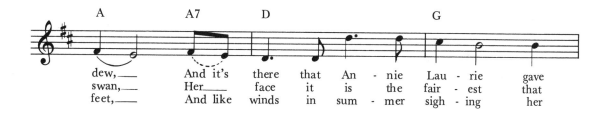

Max — well - ton braes are bon - nie, where ear - ly falls the —
brow is like the snow-drift, her neck is like the —
dew on the gow - an ly - ing is the fa' o' her fair - y —

dew, — And it's there that An - nie Lau - rie gave
swan, — Her — face it is the fair - est that
feet, — And like winds in sum - mer sigh - ing her

me her prom - ise true Gave me her prom - ise true, which
e'er the sun shone on That e'er the sun shone on, and
voice is low and sweet Her voice is low and sweet, and she's

ne'er for - got will be; } And for bon - nie bon - nie An - nie
dark blue is her e'e; }
a' the world to me; }

Laur - ie I'd — lay — me doon and dee. (2) Her dee.
(3) Like

WEE COOPER O' FIFE

Traditional

1. There was a wee coo - per who lived___ in Fife {
2. Wad - na bake, nor she wad - na brew }

Nick - e - ty, nack - e - ty noo, noo, noo { and he has got - ten a
for the spoil - ing o' her }

gen - tle wife {
come - ly hue } Hey wil - ly Wal - lack - y, noo John Dou - gal, a -

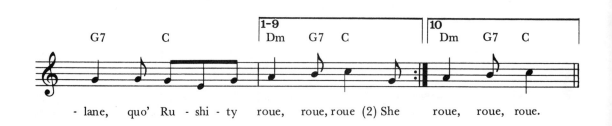

- lane, quo' Ru - shi - ty roue, roue, roue (2) She roue, roue, roue.

3. She wadna card, nor she wadna spin,
   Nickety, Nackety, noo, noo, noo,
   For the shamin' o' her gentle kin'
   Hey Willy Wallacky, hoo John Dougal,
   Alane, quo' Rushity,roue, roue.

4. She wadna wash, noe she wadna wring,
   Nickety, Nackety, noo, noo, noo,
   For the spoilin' o' her gowden ring,
   Hey Willy, Wallacky, hoo John Dougal,
   Alane, quo' Rushity,roue, roue, roue.

5. The cooper has gane to his woo' pack,
   Nickety, Nackety, noo, noo, noo,
   And he's laid a sheep's skin on his wife's back,
   Hey Willy Wallacky, hoo John Dougal,
   Alane, quo' Rushity,roue, roue, roue.

6. It's I'll no thrash ye for your gentle kin,
   Nickety, Nackety, noo, noo, noo,
   But I will thrash my ain sheep's skin,
   Hey Willy Wallacky, hoo John Dougal,
   Alane, quo' Rushity,roue, roue, roue.

7. O I will bake, and I will brew,
   Nickety, Nackety, noo, noo, noo,
   And nae mair think o' my comely hue,
   Hey Willy Wallacky, hoo John Dougal,
   Alane quo' Rushity,roue, roue, roue.

8. O I will card, and I will spin,
   Nickety, Nackety, noo, noo, noo,
   And nae mair think o' my gentle kin
   Hey Willy Wallacky, hoo John Dougal,
   Alane quo' Rushity,roue, roue, roue.

9. O I will wash, and I will wring,
   Nickety, Nackety, noo, noo, noo,
   And nae mair think o' my gowden ring,
   Hey Willy Wallacky, hoo John Dougal,
   Alane quo' Rushity,roue, roue, roue.

Moral:—

10.A' ye wha ha'e gotten a gentle wife,
   Nickety, Nackety, noo, noo, noo,
   Just you send for the wee cooper o' Fife,
   Hey Willy Wallacky, hoo John Dougal,
   Alane quo' Rushity,roue, roue, roue.

WEE WILLIE WINKIE

Traditional

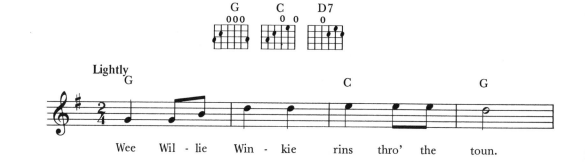

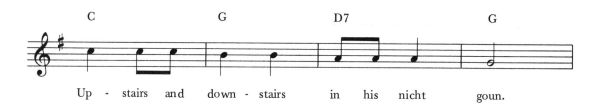

Wee Wil - lie Win - kie rins thro' the toun.

Up - stairs and down - stairs in his nicht goun.

Tir - lin' at the win - dow, cry - ing at the lock, "Are

all the bair - nies in their bed, It's past eight o' clock."

2. 'Hey Willie Winkie, are ye comin' ben?
   The cat's singin' grey thrums to the sleepin' hen,
   The dog's speldert on the floor and disna gie a cheep,
   But here's a waukrife laddie that winna fa' asleep.

3. Onything but sleep, you rogue, glow'ring like the moon,
   Rattlin' in an airn jug wi' an airn spoon,
   Rumblin', tumblin' roon about, crawin' like a cock,
   Skirlin' like I kenna what, waukenin' sleepin' folk.

4. Hey Willie Winkie, the wean's in a creel,
   Wamblin' aff a bodie's knee like a verra eel,
   Ruggin' at the cat's lug and ravellin' a' her thrums—
   Hey Willie Winkle! See, here he comes!'

THE SILKIE

Traditional

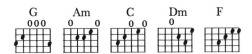

Slowly and gently

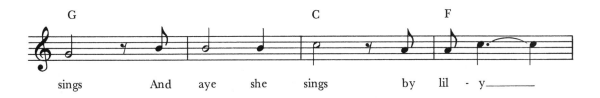

An earth-ly nurse___ sits___ and

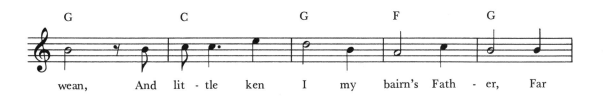

sings And aye she sings by lil-y___

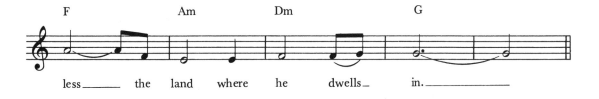

wean, And lit-tle ken I my bairn's Fath-er, Far

less___ the land where he dwells___ in.___

2. He came ae nicht tae her bed feet,
   And a grumbly guest I'm sure was he,
   Saying here am I, thy bairn's father,
   Though I am not comely be.

3. 'I am a man upon the land,
   I am a silkie in the sea,
   And when I'm far and far frae lan',
   My home it is in Sule Skerrie,'

4. And he his ta'en a purse of gowd,
   And he his pit it on her knee,
   Saying, 'Gie to me my little young son,
   And tak' thee up thy nurse's fee.

5. 'Shall come tae pass ae Simmer's day,
   When sun shines bright on every stane,
   I'll come and fetch my little young son,
   And teach him how to swim the faem.

6. 'And ye shall marry a gunner good,
   And a richt fine gunner I'm sure he'll be,
   And the very first shot that e'er he shoots,
   Will kill baith my young son and me.'

Up In The Morning Early

Traditional

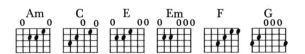

Moderately slow

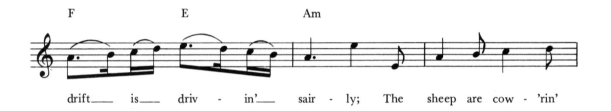

1. Cauld blaws the wind frae north___ to south, The

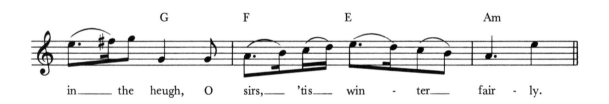

drift___ is___ driv - in'___ sair - ly; The sheep are cow - 'rin'

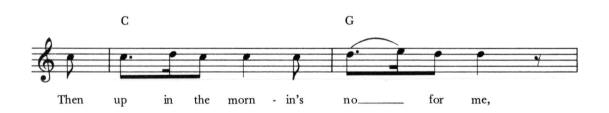

in_____ the heugh, O sirs,___ 'tis___ win - ter___ fair - ly.

Then up in the morn - in's no_____ for me,

Up in the morn - in'___ ear - ly; I'd rath - er go sup - per-less

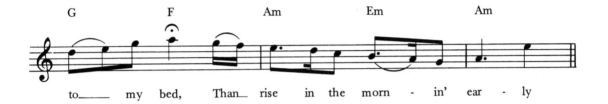

G   F   Am   Em   Am

to___ my bed, Than_ rise in the morn - in' ear - ly

2. The sun peeps owre yon southland hills
   Like any timorous carlie (fellow);
   Just blinks a wee, then sinks again,
   An' that we find severely,
   Now up in the mornin's no for me,
   Up in the mornin' early;
   When snaw blaws in at the chimley cheek,
   Who'd rise in the mornin' early?

3. A cosy house and cantie (cheerful) wife
   Aye, keep a body cheerly;
   An' pantries stowed wi' meat an' drink,
   They answer unco (strangely) rarely.
   But up in the mornin' — na, na, na!
   Up in the mornin' early;
   The gowans maun glent (daisies must shine) on bank an' brae,
   When I rise in the mornin' early.

THE FALLEN CHIEF

Traditional

Lament (Guitar tacet)

Aiken Drum

Traditional

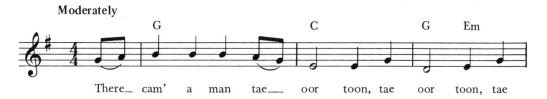

There cam' a man tae oor toon, tae oor toon, tae

oor toon, There cam' a man tae oor toon, And they ca'd him Aik-en Drum. And he

play-ed upon a la-dle a la-dle, a la-dle, And he

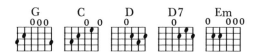

played up-on a la-dle, And his name was Aik-en Drum.

2. And his hat was made o' the guid roast beef,
the guid roast beef, the guid roast beef.
And his hat was made o' the guid roast beef,
and his name was Aiken Drum.

3. And his coat was made o' the haggis bag,
the haggis bag, the haggis bag.
And his coat was made o' the haggis bag,
and his name was Aiken Drum.

4. And his buttons were made o' the bawbee baps,
the bawbee baps, the bawbee baps.
And his buttons were made o' the bawbee baps,
and his name was Aiken Drum.

BARBARA ALLAN
Traditional

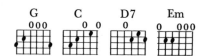

1. In Scot - land I was born— and bred, In Lon - don I was dwel - ling; I fell in love wi' a

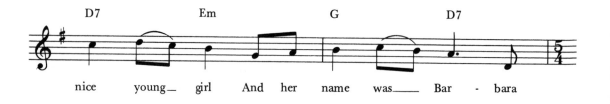

nice young— girl And her name was— Bar - bara

Al - lan, Al - lan, And her name was— Bar - bara Al - lan.

2. I courted her for seven long years,
   Till I could court no longer;
   I grew sick and very very ill,
   I sent for my own true lover, lover,
   I sent for my own true lover.

3. Slowly she put on her clothes,
   And slowly she came walking
   And when she came to my bedside
   She said, 'Young man, you are dying, dying,'
   She said, 'Young man, you are dying,'

4. 'Dying my love, that cannot be,
   One kiss from you would cure me;'
   'One kiss from me that never shall be,
   While your hard heart lies aching, aching,
   While your hard heart lies aching.'

5. He turned his back towards the wall,
   And his face to Barbara Allan,
   Adieu to you, and adieu to all,
   And adieu to Barbara Allan, Allan
   And adieu to Barbara Allen.

6. Look ye up to my bedside,
   There you will see hanging,
   A guinea gold watch and a silver chain
   And give that to Barbara Allan, Allan,
   And give that to Barbara Allan.

7. Look ye down to my bedside,
   There ye will see standing,
   A china basin full of tears,
   And give that to Barbara Allan, Allan,
   And give that to Barbara Allan.

8. She had not gone a mile or two
   When she heard the church bells tolling,
   And every toll it seemed to say —
   'Hard-hearted Barbara Allan, Allan,
   Hard-hearted Barbara Allan.

9. 'Oh mother, you'll make my bed for me
   You will make it soft and narrow;
   My love has died for me today,
   And I for him to-morrow, morrow,
   And I for him to-morrow.'

10. Her mother then she made her bed
    Wi' muckle grief and sorrow;
    She laid her down to rise no more,
    And she died for her own true lover, lover
    And she died for her own true lover.

I Know Where I'm Goin'

Words & Music by Herbert Hughes

Moderately with feeling

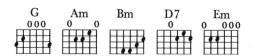

I know where I'm go - ing and I know who's go - ing with me,

I know who I love, But the lord knows who'll I'll mar - ry.

I have stock - ings of silk, and shoes of bright green leath - er,

combs to put in my hair and a ring for ev - 'ry fin - ger.

2. Feather beds are soft and painted rooms are bonny,
But I would trade them all for a walk with handsome Johnny.
Some say he is bad, but I say he is bonny,
Fairest of them all, is my handsome, winsome Johnny.

THE SKYE BOAT SONG

Traditional

Slowly, but rhythmically

Chorus: Speed bon-nie boat, like a bird on the wing, On-ward the sail-ors cry!

Car-ry the lad that is born to be king, O-ver the sea to Skye! Skye!

Verse: Loud the winds howl, Loud the waves roar, thun-der-claps rend the air,

Baf-fled our foes stand on the shore, Fol-low they will not dare.

2. Though the waves leap, soft shall ye sleep,
Ocean's a royal bed;
Rocked in the deep, Flora will keep
Watch by your weary head.

CHORUS

3. Many's the lad fought on that day,
Well the claymore could wield
When the night came, silently lay
Dead on Culloden's field.

CHORUS

4. Burned are our homes, exile and death
Scatter the loyal men;
Yet, e'er the sword cool in the sheath,
Charlie will come again.

CHORUS

THE GYPSY LADDIE

Traditional

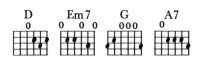

Moderately

There were three gyp - sies a' in a row, And O but they were

bon - nie - O; They sang so sweet and so com - plete That they

charmed the heart o' a la - dy O.

2. The lady she cam' doon the stair
And her twa maidens cam' wi' her O;
But when they spied her weel-faured face,
They cast their comprolls o'er her O.

3. They've gi'en to her the nutmeg fine,
   And they've gi'en to her the ginger O;
   But she's gi'en to them a far better thing,
   The gold ring aff her finger O.

4. 'It's ye'll cast aff your silken goon,
   And put on this tartan pladie O;
   And ye'll come awa' this lee-lang nicht
   And follow the gypsie laddie O.'

5. Lord Castles he cam' hame at e'en,
   Enquiring for his lady O;
   'The hounds is run and the hawk is flown,
   And the gypsy's awa' wi' your lady O.'

6. 'Come saddle me to the black, the black.
   Mak' haste and soon be ready O;
   For it's meat and drink I winna taste,
   Till I get back my lady O.'

7. They've rode east and they've rode west,
   Till them cam' to yonder boggie O;
   And there they spied the weel-faured maid,
   Wi the gypsies a' standin' roond her O.

8. 'Will ye gang wi' me, my honey and my heart,
   Will ye gang wi' me, my lady O;
   And I swear by the sword that hangs by my side,
   The black band shall never steal thee O.'

9. 'I winna come wi' you, my honey and my heart,
   I winna come wi' you, my dearie O;
   Till I hae drunk the breest I brewed,
   And that's in the water o' Eerie O.'

GREEN GROW THE RASHES-O

Traditional

Moderately

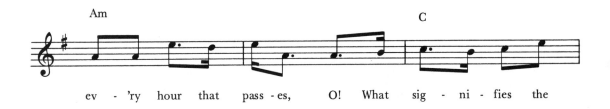

1. There's nought but care on ev - 'ry han', In

ev - 'ry hour that pass - es, O! What sig - ni - fies the

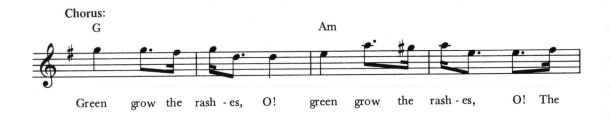

life o' man, An' 'twere na' for the lass - es, O?

Chorus:

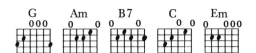

Green grow the rash - es, O! green grow the rash - es, O! The

sweet - est hours that e'er I spend Are spent a - mong the lass - es, O!

2. The warldly (worldly) race may riches chase,
    An' riches still may fly them, O;
    An' though at last they catch them fast,
    Their hearts can ne'er enjoy them, O!

CHORUS

3. Gie me a cantie (cheerful) hour at e'en.
    My arms about my dearie, O:
    An' warldly cares and warldly men
    May a' gae tapsalteerie, O (topsy-turvy).

CHORUS

4. And you sae douce (wise, or sober) wha sneer at this,
    Ye're nought but sensless asses, O!
    The wisest man the warld e'er saw,
    He dearly lo'ed the lasses, O.

CHORUS

5. Auld Nature swears the lovely dears
    Her noblest works she classes, O:
    Her 'prentice han' she tried on man,
    An' then she made the lasses, O.

CHORUS

Down In The Glen

Words & Music by Harry Gordon & Tommie Connor

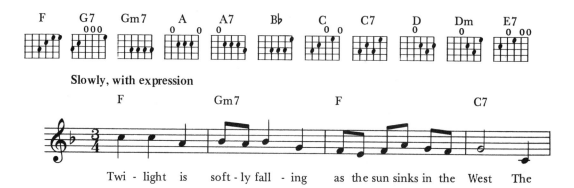

Slowly, with expression

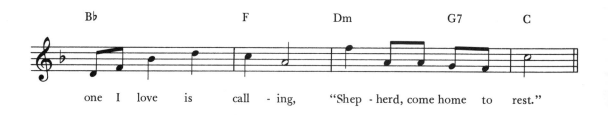

Twi - light is soft - ly fall - ing as the sun sinks in the West The

one I love is call - ing, "Shep - herd, come home to rest."

Chorus:

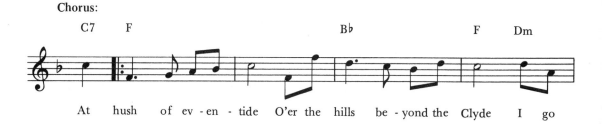

At hush of ev - en - tide O'er the hills be - yond the Clyde I go

roam - ing to my hea - ven Down in the glen. Though hum - ble it may

be, There an an - gel waits for me In that lone - ly, lit - tle hea - ven,

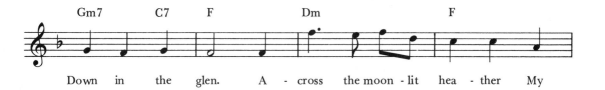

Down in the glen. A - cross the moon - lit hea - ther My

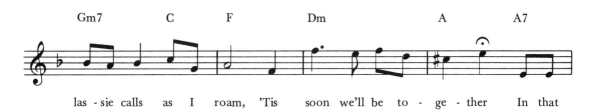

las - sie calls as I roam, 'Tis soon we'll be to - ge - ther In that

hea - ven we call "home." The sheep are in the fold And there's

peace worth more than gold, For a shep - herd in that hea - ven

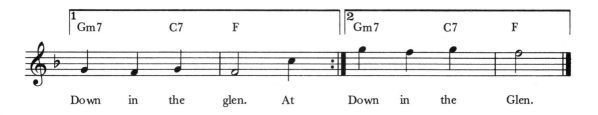

Down in the glen. At Down in the Glen.

WATERLOO HORNPIPE
Traditional

BONNIE LADDIE, HIGHLAND LADDIE

Traditional

Where ha'e ye been a' the day, Bon - nie lad - die

High - land lad - die? Saw ye him that's far a - way,

Bon - nie lad - die high - land lad - die? On his head a

bon - net blue, Bon - nie lad - die High-land lad - die, Tar - tan plaid and

High - land trew Bon - nie lad - die, High - land lad - die!

2. When he drew his gude braid (good broad) sword
   Bonnie laddie, highland laddie,
   Then he gave his royal word,
   Bonnie laddie, highland laddie,
   That frae the field he ne'r would flee,
   Bonnie laddie, highland laddie;
   But wi' his friends would live or dee,
   Bonnie laddie, highland laddie.

BONNY MARY OF ARGYLE

Traditional

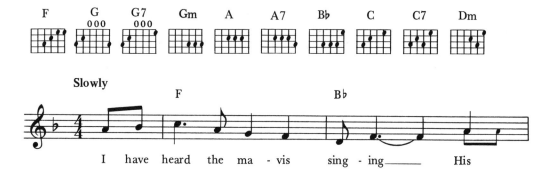

I have heard the ma - vis sing - ing____ His

love song to the morn; I have seen the dew - drop

cling - ing____ To the rose just new - ly born. But a

sweet - er song has cheer'd me At the ev - 'ning's gen - tle

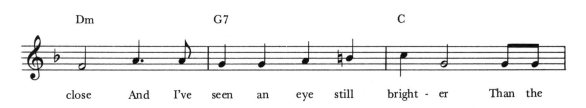

close And I've seen an eye still bright - er Than the

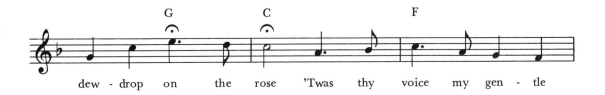

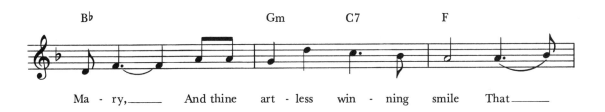

dew - drop on the rose 'Twas thy voice my gen - tle

Ma - ry,_____ And thine art - less win - ning smile That_____

made this world an E - den, Bon - ny Ma - ry of__ Ar - gyle.

2. Tho' thy voice may lose its sweetness
And thine eye its brightness too,
Tho' thy step may lack its fleetness,
And thy hair its sunny hue,
Still to me wilt thou be dearer,
Than all the world shall own.
I have loved thee for thy beauty
But not for that alone.
I have sought thy heart, dear Mary,
And its goodness was the wile
That has made thee mine forever
Bonny Mary of Argyle.

LOCH LOMOND

Traditional

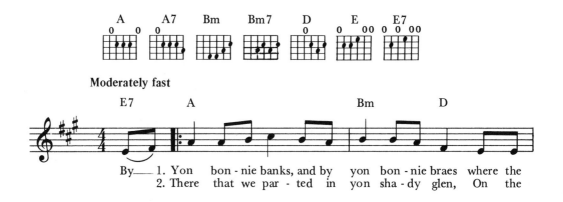

Moderately fast

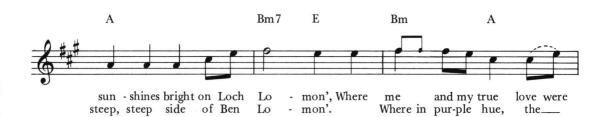

By— 1. Yon bon - nie banks, and by yon bon - nie braes where the
2. There that we par - ted in yon sha - dy glen, On the

sun - shines bright on Loch Lo - mon', Where me and my true love were
steep, steep side of Ben Lo - mon'. Where in pur - ple hue, the—

e - ver won't to gae, On the bon - nie bon - nie banks o' Loch Lo - mon'.{ Oh—
hie - lan' hills we view, An' the moon com - in' out in the gloam - in'

You tak' the high road, and I'll tak' the low road, An' I'll be in Scot - land a -

fore ye, But me and my true love will nev-er meet a-gain On the

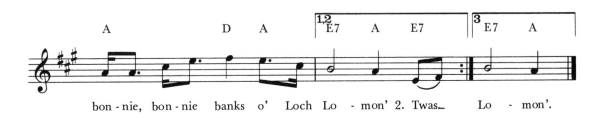

bon-nie, bon-nie banks o' Loch Lo - mon' 2. Twas_ Lo - mon'.

3. The wee birdies sing, and the wild flowers spring,
   While in sunshine the waters are sleepin',
   But the broken heart it kens nae spring again,
   Tho' the waefu' may cease frae their greetin'
   Oh you tak' the high road, *etc.*

THE BORDER LAMENT

Traditional

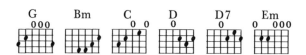

1. My love he built me a bon - nie bow'r, And clad it a' wi' li - lye flow'r, A braw - er bow'r ye

ne'er did see, Than my true love he built for me.

2. There came a man by middle day,
   He spied his sport, and went away,
   And brought the king that very night,
   Who brake my bow'r and slew my knight.

3. He slew my knight, to me sae dear,
   He slew my knight, and pin'd his gear;
   The servants all for life did flee,
   And left me in extremitie.

4. I took his body on my back,
   And while I gaed, and while I sate;
   I digg'd a grave, and laid him in,
   And happ'd him with the sod sae green.

I'M A ROVER

Traditional

Vigorously

1. I'm a ro-ver and sel-dom so-ber, I'm a ro-ver o' high de-gree; It's when I'm drink-ing I'm al-ways think-ing How to gain my love's com-pa-ny.

2. Though the nicht be as dark as dungeon,
   No' a star to be seen above,
   I will be guided without a stumble
   Into the airms o' my ain true love.

3. He steppit up to her bedroom window,
   Kneelin' gently upon a stone,
   He rappit at her bedroom window:
   'Darlin' dear, do you lie alone?'

4. She raised her head on her snaw white pillow,
   Wi' her airms aboot her breast,
   'Wha' is that at my bedroom window,
   Disturbing me at my lang night's rest?'

5. 'It's only me, your ain true lover;
   Open the door and let me in,
   For I hae come on a lang journey
   And I'm near drenched unto the skin.'

6. She opened the door wi' the greatest pleasure,
   She opened the door and let him in.
   They baith shook hands and embraced each other,
   Until the morning they lay as one.

7. The cocks were crawin', the birds were whistlin',
   The burns they ran free abune the brae:
   'Remember lass I'm a ploughman laddie
   And the fairmer I must obey.

8. 'Noo ma love, I must go and leave you,
   Tae climb the hills, thay are far above;
   But I will climb them wi' the greatest pleasure,
   Since I've been in the airms o' ma love.'

MacPherson's Farewell

Traditional

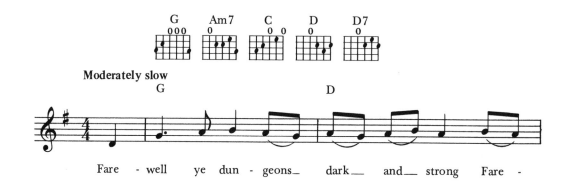

Moderately slow

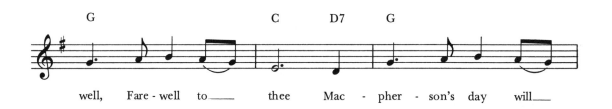

Fare - well ye dun - geons_ dark_ and_ strong Fare -

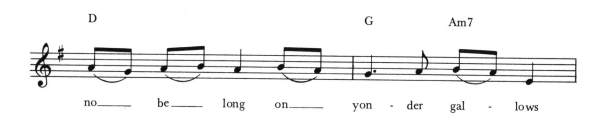

well, Fare - well to_ thee Mac - pher - son's day will_

no_ be_ long on_ yon - der gal - lows

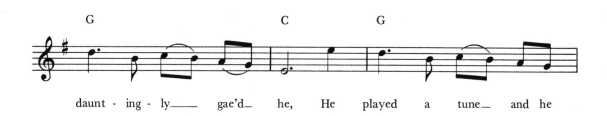

tree Sae_ rant - ing - ly_ sae_ want - on - ly and sae

daunt - ing - ly_ gae'd_ he, He played a tune_ and he

danced it roond A - bout the gal - lows tree.

2. 'It was by a woman's treacherous hand
   That I was condemned to die.
   Below a ledge at a window she stood
   And a blanket she threw over me.

3. There's some come here to see me die
   And some to buy my fiddle.
   But before that I do part with her,
   I'll break her down the middle.'

4. He took the fiddle into both his hands
   And broke it o'er a stone.
   Said 'There's no other hand shall play on thee,
   When I am dead and gone.

5. O little did my mother think
   When first she cradled me,
   That I would turn a roving boy
   And die on the gallows tree.'

6. The reprieve was coming o'er the brig o' Banff
   To let Macpherson free.
   But they put the clock at a quarter afore
   And hanged him on the tree.

THE FLOWERS OF EDINBURGH

Traditional

THE BLUEBELLS OF SCOTLAND

Traditional

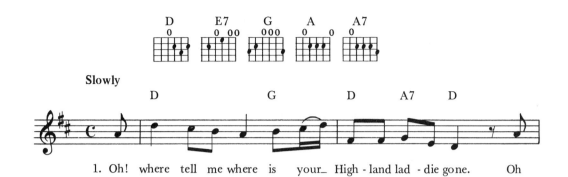

Slowly

1. Oh! where tell me where is your_ High - land lad - die gone. Oh

where tell me where is your_ High-land lad-die gone. He's gone with stream-ing ban-ners, where_

no - ble deeds are done, And my sad heart will trem - ble till_ he comes safe-ly hame.

2. Oh where, tell me where, did your Highland laddie stay?
   Oh where, tell me where, did your Highland laddie stay?
   He dwelt beneath the holly trees beside the rapid Spey?
   And many a blessing followed him the day he went away.

3. Oh what, tell me what, does your Highland laddie wear?
   Oh what, tell me what, does your Highland laddie wear?
   A bonnet with a lofty plume, the gallant badge of war,
   And a plaid across his manly breast that yet shall wear a star.

4. Suppose, ah suppose, that some cruel, cruel wound
   Should pierce your Highland laddie and all your hopes confound;
   The pipe would play a cheering march the banners round him fly,
   And for his kind and country dear with pleasure would he die.

Charlie Is My Darlin'

Traditional

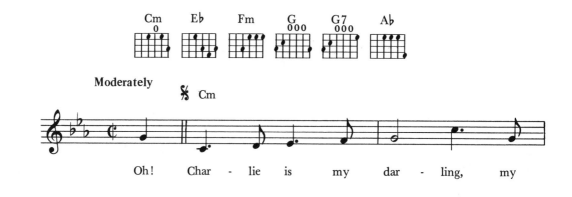

Moderately

Oh! Char - lie is my dar - ling, my

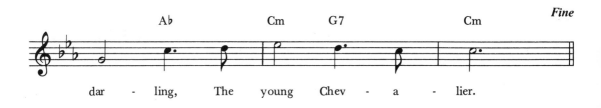

dar - ling, my dar - ling, Oh! Char - lie is my

dar - ling, The young Chev - a - lier.

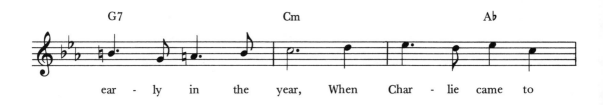

1. 'Twas on a Mon - day morn - ing, Right

ear - ly in the year, When Char - lie came to

our_____ town, The____ young__ Chev - a - lier. Oh!

2. As he cam' marchin' up the street,
   The pipes play'd loud and clear,
   And a' the folk cam' rinnin' out
   To meet the Chevalier. Oh!

CHORUS

3. Wi' Hieland bonnets on their heads,
   And claymores bright and clear;
   They cam' to fight for Scotland's right
   And the young Chevalier. Oh!

CHORUS

4. They've left their bonnie Hieland hills,
   Their wives and bairnies dear,
   To draw the sword for Scotland's lord,
   The young Chevalier. Oh!

CHORUS

ON THE BANKS OF ALLAN WATER

Traditional

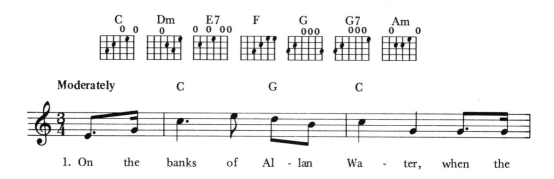

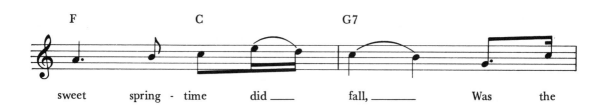

1. On the banks of Al - lan Wa - ter, when the

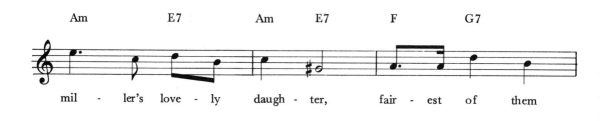

sweet spring - time did ___ fall, _____ Was the

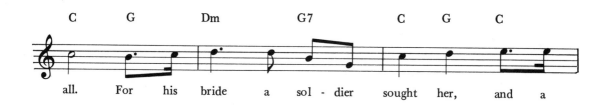

mil - ler's love - ly daugh - ter, fair - est of them

all. For his bride a sol - dier sought her, and a

2. On the banks of Allan Water,
   When brown autumn spreads its store,
   There I saw the miller's daughter,
   But she smiled no more.
   For the summer grief had brought her,
   And the soldier false was he;
   On the banks of Allan Water.
   None so sad as she.

3. On the banks of Allan Water,
   When the winter snow fell fast,
   Still was seen the miller's daughter;
   Chilling blew the blast.
   But the miller's lovely daughter
   Both from cold and care was free.
   On the banks of Allan Water
   There a corpse lay she.

Wi' A Hundred Pipers

Traditional

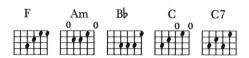

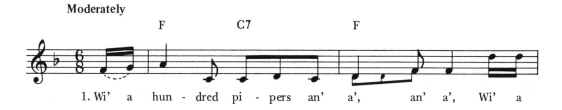

Moderately

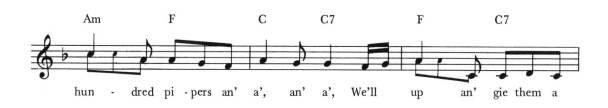

1. Wi' a hun - dred pi - pers an' a', an' a', Wi' a

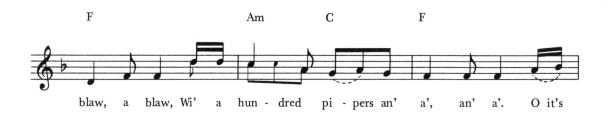

hun - dred pi - pers an' a', an' a', We'll up an' gie them a

blaw, a blaw, Wi' a hun - dred pi - pers an' a', an' a'. O it's

ow - re the bor - der a - wa', a - wa', It's__ ow - re the bor - der a -

- wa', a - wa', We'll__ on an' we'll march - to Car - lisle ha', Wi' its

yetts', its cas-tle an' a', an' a'. Wi' a hun-dred pi-pers an'

a', an' a', Wi a hun-dred pi-pers an' a' an', a', We'll_ up an' gie them a

blaw, a blaw, Wi a hun-dred pi-pers an' a', an' a'. Wi' a a', an' a'.

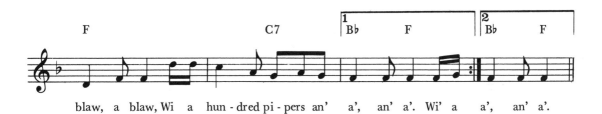

2. Oh! our sodger lads looked braw, looked braw,
   Wi' their tartan kilts an'a, an'a,
   Wi' their bonnets an' feathers an' glitt'rin' gear,
   An' pibrochs sounding loud and clear.
   Will they a' return to their ain dear glen?
   Will they a' return oor Heilan' men?
   Second sichted Sandy looked fu' wae.
   An' mithers grat when march'd away.

CHORUS

3. Oh! wha is foremost o' a', o' a',
   Oh! wha is foremost o' a', o' a',
   Bonnie Charlie the King o' us a', hurrah!
   Wi' his hundred pipers an' a', an' a'.
   His bonnet and feathers he's waving high,
   His prancing steed maist seems to fly,
   The nor' win' plays wi' his curly hair,
   While the pipers play wi' an unco flare.

CHORUS

4. The Esk was swollen sae red an' sae deep,
   But shouther to shouther the brave lads keep;
   Twa thousand swam owre to fell English ground
   An' danced themselves dry to the pibroch's sound
   Dumfoun'er'd the English saw, they saw,
   Dumfoun'er'd they heard the blaw, the blaw,
   Dumfoun'er'd they a' ran awa', awa',
   Frae the hundred pipers an' a', an' a'.

CHORUS

Ye Banks And Braes

Traditional

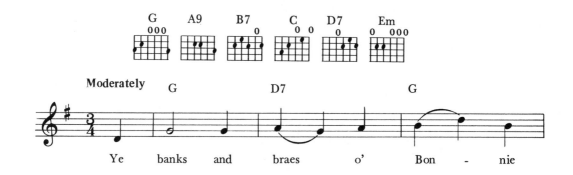

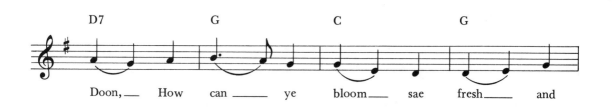

Ye banks and braes o' Bon - nie

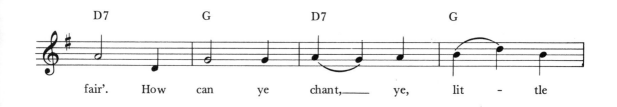

Doon, __ How can __ ye bloom __ sae fresh __ and

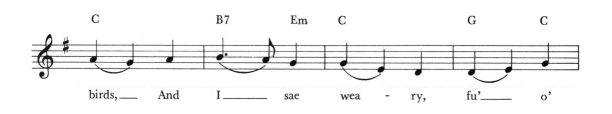

fair'. How can ye chant, __ ye, lit - tle

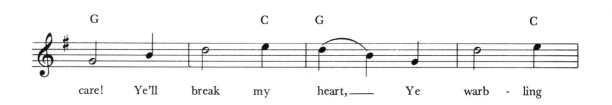

birds, __ And I __ sae wea - ry, fu' __ o'

care! Ye'll break my heart, __ Ye warb - ling

bird, That wan - tons thro' the flow'r - ing thorn; Ye

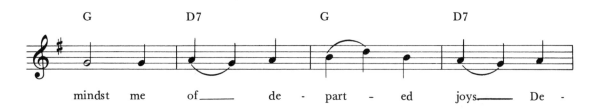

mindst me of____ de - part - ed joys.____ De -

- part - ed, nev - er to____ re - turn.

2. Oft have I roved by Bonnie Doon,
   To see the rose and woodbine twine;
   And ilka bird sang o' its love,
   And fondly sae did I o' mine.
   Wi' light-some heart, I pu'd a rose,
   Fu' sweet upon its thorny tree;
   And my fause lover stole my rose,
   But ah! he left the thorn wi' me.

THE COLLIER LADDIE

Traditional

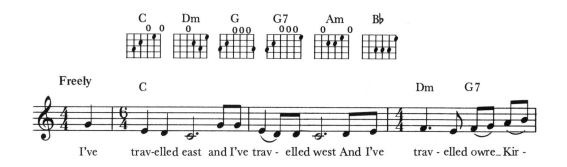

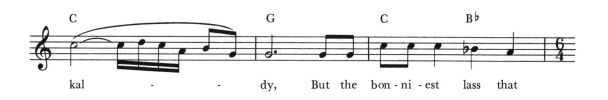

I've trav-elled east and I've trav-elled west And I've trav-elled owre Kir-

kal - - dy, But the bon-ni-est lass that

e'er I spied, She was fol-low-in' her col - lier lad - die.

Chorus:

Lad - die, O lad - - die, But the bon-ni-est lass that

e'er I spied, She was fol-low-in' her col - lier lad - die.

2. 'O whaur live ye my bonnie lass?
   Come tell me what they ca' ye.'
   'Bonnie Jean Gordon is my name,
   And I'm followin' a collier laddie.'

CHORUS

3. 'O would ye fancy ane that's black
   And you sae fair and gaudy?
   O fancy ane o' higher degree,
   Than followin' a collier laddie.'

CHORUS

4. 'Ye see yon hills the sun shines on,
   The sun shines on sae gaudy;
   They a' are mine and they shall be thine,
   Gin ye'll leave your collier laddie.'

CHORUS

5. 'Though ye had a' the sun shines on,
   And the earth conceals sae lowly,
   I wad turn my back on you and it a'
   And follow my collier laddie.'

CHORUS

6. Then he has gane to her faither dear,
   To her faither gane sae brawly;
   Says: 'Will ye gie me your bonnie, bonnie lass
   That's followin' a collier laddie?

CHORUS

7. 'O would she marry a man that's black,
   And me sea braw and gaudy?
   I'll raise her up to a higher degree
   Than followin' a collier laddie.'

CHORUS

8. Her faither then he vowed and swore:
   'Though he be black he's bonnie;
   She's mair delight in him, I fear,
   Than in you wi' a' your money.'

CHORUS

9. 'O I can win my five pennies a day,
   And spend't at nicht fu' brawly,
   And I'll mak' my bed in the collier's neuk
   And lie doon wi' my collier laddie.

CHORUS

10. 'Love for love is the bargain for me,
    Though the wee cot-hoose should haud me,
    And the world before me to win my breid,
    And fare for my collier laddie.

CHORUS

THE BREWER LAD

Traditional

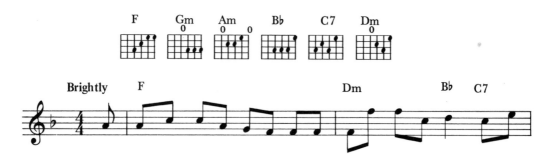

1. In Perth there lived a bon-nie lad, A brew-er tae his trade, oh; And

he has cour-ted Peg-gie Roy, A young and hand-some maid, oh. Wi' a

fal dal did-dle um a die dum doo, Wi' a fal dal did-dle um a die doh.

2. He courted her for seiven lang years,
   A' for to gain her favour;
   But there cam' a lad oot o' Edinburgh toon,
   Wha swore that he would have her.

3. "It's will ye gang alang wi' me,
   And will ye be my honey;
   It's will ye gang alang wi' me,
   And leave your brewer laddie?"

4. "Oh, I will gang alang wi' you,
   And alang wi' you I'll ride, oh;
   I'll gang wi' you to the ends o' the earth,
   Tho' I'm spoke to the brewer lad, oh."

5. The brewer he cam' hame at e'en,
   A-speirin' for his honey;
   Her faither he made this reply:
   "She's no' been here since Monday."

6. Oh, wasna that an unco ploy,
   Wouldna anyone been offended?
   To court wi' a lad for seiven years
   And leave him at the end o't.

7. "Oh, be it so and let her go,
   For it shall never grieve me;
   I'm a lad that's free, as you can see,
   And a sma' thing will relieve me.

8. "There's as guid fish intae the sea,
   As ever yet was taken;
   I'll cast my net and try again,
   Although I am forsaken."

9. She's rambled up, she's rambled doon,
   She's rambled through Kirkcaldie,
   And mony's the time she's rued the day,
   She jilted her brewer laddie.

10. He's ta'en his course and away he's gane,
    The country he has fled, oh;
    And he's left nae sark upon her back,
    Nor blanket on her bed, oh.

11. The brewer lad set up in Perth,
    And there he brews strong ale, oh;
    And he has courted anither lass,
    And ta'en her tae himsel', oh.

12. Ye lovers a', where'er ye be,
    Just let this be a warning;
    And never slight your ain true love,
    For fear ye get a waur ane.

EAST NEUK O' FIFE

Traditional

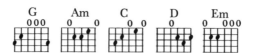

Rhythmically

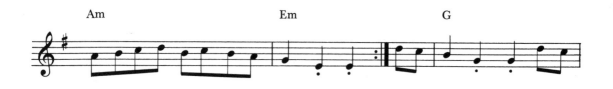

MY LOVE IS LIKE A RED RED ROSE

Traditional

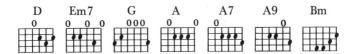

Slowly, with feeling

My love is like a red, red rose that's
A' the seas gang dry, my dear, and the

new-ly sprung in June, My_ love is like a mel-o-dy that's sweet-ly played in tune. As
rocks meet with the sun, And_ I will love thee still, my dear, while the sands of life shall run. But

fair art thou, my bon-nie lass, so deep in love am I____ And____
fare-thee-well my on-ly love! oh fare-thee-well a while!_ And____

I will love thee still, my dear till a' the seas gang dry; Till
I will come a-gain, my love, tho' 'twere ten thous-and miles. Tho'

a' the seas gang dry, my dear, till a' the seas gang dry And____
'twere ten thous-and miles, my love, tho' 'twere ten thous-and miles, And____

I will love thee still my dear, Till a' the seas gang dry. (2) Till
I will come a-gain, my love, Tho'   'twere ten thous-and miles.

AULD LANG SYNE

Traditional

Moderately, with expression

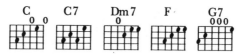

Should auld ac - quain - tance be for - got and___
(And) there's a hand, my trust - y friend, and___

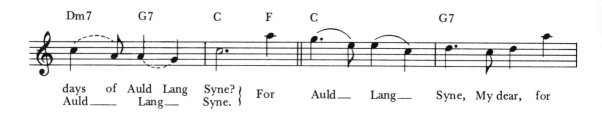

nev - er brought to mind? Should auld ac - quain-tance be for - got, and___
gie's a hand in thine. We'll tak' a right gude wil - ly waught, for___

days of Auld Lang Syne? } For Auld___ Lang___ Syne, My dear, for
Auld___ Lang___ Syne.

Auld___ Lang___ Syne, We'll take a cup of

kind - ness yet, for___ Auld___ Lang___ Syne. (2) And Syne.